Everybody! Babies!

BETH WILLIAMS-BREAULT

Tellwell Talent
www.tellwell.ca

ISBN
978-0-2288-3856-2 (Hardcover)
978-0-2288-3855-5 (Paperback)

This book is dedicated to my children, Griffin and Macy.
"Always do your best. What you plant now, you will harvest later."
-Og Mandino

Mommy and baby go for a walk in the park.

There are mommies with babies. Daddies with babies.

Some babies have a big brother. Some have a big sister. Some don't.

Babies always have a grown-up.

Grown-ups, babies, and kids make a family. Pets, too.

Many families come from different countries and speak different languages.

Mommy explains that everybody was a baby.

Grown-ups take care of babies and kids. Kids help take care of babies, too.

Families come in many different colors, shapes, and sizes.

A family loves each other!